STUDY GUIDE

THE

DAY

APPROACHING

AMIR TSARFATI

HARVEST PROPHECY
AN IMPRINT OF HARVEST HOUSE PUBLISHERS

is a trademark of The Hawkins Children's LLC. Harvest House Publishers, Inc., is the exclusive licensee of the trademark.

The Day Approaching Study Guide
Copyright © 2020 by Amir Tsarfati
Published by Harvest House Publishers
Eugene, Oregon 97408
www.harvesthousepublishers.com

ISBN 978-0-7369-8109-5 (pbk.)
ISBN 978-0-7369-8110-1 (eBook)

Printed in the United States of America

21 22 23 24 25 / BP-CD / 10 9 8 7 6 5

CONTENTS

CHAPTER 1

ANY DAY NOW

> "I have no clue as to the day and time of Christ's return. But I'm in good company. No person knows the day and time. The angels don't know. Not even the Son of God Himself knows. Jesus said, "Of that day and hour no one knows, not even the angels of heaven, but My Father only" (Matthew 24:36). The Father has got the timing planned out to the minute, but He's keeping His cards close to His chest. What I can tell you is that as I look at the events unfolding in the world around us, I firmly believe that the day of Jesus' return is rapidly approaching."
>
> *The Day Approaching,* page 10

While we cannot know when Jesus will return, we can know with absolute certainty that He will come back. As we cling to this promise, we are challenged by scoffers who say, "Where is the promise of His coming? For since the fathers fell asleep, all things continue as they were from the beginning of creation" (2 Peter 3:4).

There are those who reason that because Jesus has not returned for 2,000 years, then either it won't happen or we're misunderstanding what he said. Some people point to Revelation 22:12, where Jesus said, "Behold, I am coming quickly," and they say, "Two thousand years have gone by, and Jesus still hasn't come back." But the Greek word translated "quickly" means "swiftly" or "at a rapid rate." In context, Jesus was saying that once the world enters the end times, events will progress speedily and His return will happen very soon.

There are hundreds of prophecies about the end times that have yet to be fulfilled, including those about Jesus' second coming. How confident can we be that they really will take place? Read the following verses and write what they tell you about God and His promises.

Deuteronomy 7:9—

1 Kings 8:56—

2 Corinthians 1:20—

Hebrews 10:23—

Hebrews 10:36-37—

What are some reasons God would want to keep "the day and hour" of Christ's return a secret?

According to the following passages, how should we live as we wait for the rapture to take place?

Matthew 25:13—

Ephesians 5:15-16—

Titus 2:11-13—

2 Peter 3:10-12—

In your own words, describe what it would be like for a Christian to live in a state of expectation and readiness. In what two or three ways can you grow in this area of your own life?

GOD WANTS YOU TO KNOW HIS PLAN

While there are some things we don't know about the end times—such as the exact moment of Christ's return—there is a lot God does reveal. When the disciples asked Jesus, "What will be the sign of Your coming, and of the end of the age?" (Matthew 24:3), the Lord didn't leave them in the dark. He shared some general details about what would happen as we approach the tribulation and second coming.

Read Matthew 24:4-28, and list at least seven of the signs Jesus said would take place:

—

—

—

—

—

—

—

After you finish reading about the signs in Matthew 24, consider what is taking place in the world today. Do you agree with those who sense that Christ's rapture of believers could happen "any day now"? Why or why not?

THE TIMES ARE MOVING FORWARD

When it comes to future events, we can separate them into two categories:

1. Those we can do something about
2. Those we can't

To what extent is God in control of the future (see Job 42:2 and Isaiah 14:27)?

Is there ever a time we can alter God's plans? What specifically does Psalm 33:11 say?

While we cannot change God's plans for the future, we can definitely choose where we will spend eternity—either with God, or apart from Him. Read 2 Corinthians 6:2-3. According to Paul, when is "the day of salvation"?

Why do you think Paul said this with such a sense of urgency?

Once we become believers, what else can we do as we wait for Christ's return, according to Hebrews 10:23-25?

"As we read the newspapers and watch the cable channels, a contrast becomes evident. On the one hand, everything seems to be falling apart…On the other hand, when we look through the lens of Scripture, everything is falling into place."

The Day Approaching, page 19

Read 2 Timothy 3:1-4. What will people be like "in the last days"?

With 2 Timothy 3:1-4 in mind, what are some specific examples of ways you've seen our world "falling apart"?

Read the following passages. With the rebirth of the nation of Israel in 1948, in what ways would you say God's plans are falling into place?

Isaiah 66:7-8—

Jeremiah 16:14-15—

Ezekiel 37:21-22—

THE SIGNS OF THE TIMES

When the disciples asked Jesus, "What will be the sign of Your coming, and of the end of the age?," Jesus mentioned these signs in his response: "Many will come in My name, saying, 'I am the Christ,' and will deceive many. And you will hear of wars and rumors of wars…For nation will rise against nation, and kingdom against kingdom. And there will be famines, pestilences, and earthquakes in various places. All these are the beginning of sorrows" (Matthew 24:3,5-8).

Looking at what is happening around the world, in what ways would you say Jesus described our times?

Matthew 24:8 says these signs "are the beginning of sorrows." The events of the end times will occur in the same fashion as labor pains—that is, as time progresses, they will increase with intensity and frequency. In what ways do you see this pattern evident around us today?

When Jesus gave His answer to the disciples, notice His personal encouragement to them: "See that you are not troubled; for all these things must come to pass" (verse 6).

Why do you think Jesus said that we, as believers, should not be troubled?

What assurance are we given when Jesus says, "All these things must come to pass"?

Read 2 Timothy 3:12-14. What did Paul say would happen to all believers, according to verse 12?

What trend can we expect, as stated in verse 13?

How are we to respond (verse 14)?

Jesus has promised to return for His church: "Let not your heart be troubled; you believe in God, believe also in me. In My Father's house are many mansions; if it were not so, I would have told you. I go to prepare a place for you. And if I go and prepare a place for you, I will come again and receive you to Myself; that where I am, there you may be also" (John 14:1-3).

We could meet Jesus in the clouds any day now. In what ways are you looking forward to this?

ABIDING IN GOD'S WORD
AS WE AWAIT CHRIST'S RETURN

> The grace of God that brings salvation has appeared to all men, teaching us that, denying ungodliness and worldly lusts, we should live soberly, righteously and godly in the present age, looking for the blessed hope and glorious appearing of our great God and Savior Jesus Christ (Titus 2:11-13).

How are we called to live in this present age?

What are we to look for?

What are some benefits we can gain from living in righteous expectation?

CHAPTER 2

THE FIG TREE AND THE FINAL GENERATION

"Jesus says that when the fig tree starts sprouting, 'you know' that it is almost summer. These are important words. You are not just hoping for the summer or longing for the summer. There is no doubt that a sprouting tree means that spring is about to move off the scene and be replaced by warmer weather. Once more, Jesus says that when you 'see' these signs, you will know that the time is near."

The Day Approaching, page 28

THE PARABLE OF THE FIG TREE

To set the context, let's begin by reading the parable:

Now learn this parable from the fig tree: When its branch has already become tender and puts

> forth leaves, you know that summer is near. So you also, when you see all these things, know that it is near—at the doors! Assuredly, I say to you, this generation will by no means pass away till all these things take place. Heaven and earth will pass away, but My words will by no means pass away (Matthew 24:32-35).

When it comes to Bible prophecy, there is much speculation about what will happen in the future. There are people who believe they have unlocked mysterious clues about the last days, yet when you take a closer look at what they teach, you discover that they are reading their own conclusions into the Bible rather than letting God's Word speak for itself.

If we want to understand the end times, there is no better place to go than to Jesus Himself. In Matthew 24, He lays out for His disciples the signs "of the end of the age" (verse 3). It is within this teaching that we find the parable of the fig tree. Here, Jesus reveals how we can know that the end is near. He also identifies the generation that will see all these things happen before the grand conclusion of human history.

HOW LONG IS A GENERATION?

The Length of a Generation

To understand this passage, it is necessary to know the answer to this question: What is a generation?

The View that a Generation Is 40 Years

After the people of Israel had made their way from Egypt to the borders of the Promised Land, spies were sent to evaluate the military threat that lay ahead. As it turned out, the people became exceedingly afraid because all the spies—except for Joshua and Caleb—said, "The land through which we have gone as spies is a land that devours its inhabitants, and all the people whom we saw in it are men of great stature...and we were like grasshoppers in our own sight" (Numbers 13:32-33).

In response to Israel's fear and refusal to enter the land, God said, "Surely none of the men who came up from Egypt, from twenty years old and above, shall see the land of which I swore to Abraham" (Numbers 32:11). As punishment, "He made them wander in the wilderness forty years, until all the generation that had done evil in the sight of the LORD was gone" (verse 13).

Based on Numbers 32, some have concluded that a generation is 40 years. But what does that view fail to take into account? (See page 31 in *The Day Approaching*.)

The View that a Generation Is a Full Life Span

In Psalm 90:9-10, Moses wrote, "All our days have passed away in Your wrath; we finished our years like a sigh. The days of our lives are seventy years; and if by reason of strength they are eighty years, yet their boast is only labor and sorrow; for it is soon cut off, and we fly away."

How long does Moses say is a full life span?

THE THREE PLANTS OF ISRAEL

The Identity of "This Generation"

Also key to understanding the parable of the fig tree is properly identifying who "this generation" is. Some say Jesus was talking about the generation who was alive at the time He taught the parable. But is that a reasonable conclusion?

The Evidence from History

The budding of a fig tree signifies new life and growth. In contrast, at the time of Jesus' ministry, Israel was under great oppression by the Roman government.

Read Matthew 22:15-22. What attitude are we able to discern among the Jewish people about the requirement to pay taxes to Caesar and Roman governing authorities?

According to John 11:48, what did the Jewish religious leaders fear would happen if too many people followed Jesus?

In Matthew 27:18, what attitude did the Jewish religious leaders show when they had to turn Jesus over to the Roman governor Pilate (because they lacked the authority to do anything to Jesus on their own)?

Clearly, the Jewish people chafed under oppressive Roman rule, so it's incorrect to conclude that "this generation"—in the parable of the fig tree—applied to those alive in Jesus' day.

The Evidence from Prophecy

Read the following verses in Matthew 24, and briefly note what they describe:

Verse 15—

Verses 17-22—

Verses 23-26—

Verses 27-29—

Verse 30—

Verse 31—

Did all the things described in the above verses come to pass for the generation who was alive at the time Jesus taught the parable of the fig tree?

Because all the events described in the above verses are still in the future, we can safely conclude that "this generation" refers to those who are alive when the birth pains in Matthew 24:6-7 take place.

"There are so many in the church who want to be the fig tree—they want to be Jews…However, if you are one of those who wishes you were Jewish, let me suggest you point your aspirations in a different direction. All you need to do is look at a little history to realize that being a Jew isn't all it's cracked up to be…

"If, as a Gentile, your desire is to be a Jew, then you are missing out on your vital role in God's plan. Paul says in Romans 11 that you are to help provoke the Jews to jealousy…the church should be showing Israel just how wonderful it is to have a close, personal relationship with God."

The Day Approaching, pages 34-35

In Romans 11:14, Paul expressed his desire to "provoke to jealousy" His fellow Jews to "save some of them." What are some of the ways that Gentile Christians can make Christ attractive to Jewish people (and everyone else, for that matter)?

THE BRANCH PUTS FORTH LEAVES

Note what Ezekiel said when he prophesied about the budding of the fig tree, or the recovery of the land of Israel:

> You, O mountains of Israel, you shall shoot forth your branches and yield your fruit to My people Israel, for they are about to come. For

> indeed I am for you, and I will turn to you, and
> you shall be tilled and sown. I will multiply men
> upon you, all the house of Israel, all of it; and
> the cities shall be inhabited and the ruins rebuilt.
> I will multiply upon you man and beast; and
> they shall increase and bear young; I will make
> you inhabited as in former times, and do better
> for you than at your beginnings. Then you shall
> know that I am the LORD (Ezekiel 36:8-11).

Below, write at least three specific promises God makes in
that prophecy.

—

—

—

What do you know about Israel today that serves as evidence
that God has brought life back to the land and nation?

"You are part of the generation that sees Israel back in the land. You are alive to see the nation flourish. You have seen this miraculous work of God...For the first time ever, we have the church and Israel living and thriving at the same time."

The Day Approaching, page 37

A ROCK-SOLID NONPREDICTION

Matthew 24:36 makes it clear that it is impossible to predict exactly when Christ will return: "Of that day and hour no one knows, not even the angels of heaven, but My Father only."

A little later, however—in verse 44—Jesus gives us a specific command. What does He ask us to do?

ABIDING IN GOD'S WORD
AS WE AWAIT CHRIST'S RETURN

> You also be ready, for the Son of Man is coming
> at an hour you do not expect (Matthew 24:44).

As we watch and wait, we are to be doing our Father's business. What would that look like in your life with regard to...

Your responses to temptation and sin?

Your attitudes?

Your personal stewardship of what God has entrusted to you?

Your interactions with fellow believers?

Your interactions with unbelievers?

Your role as a part of the body of Christ at your church?

Your prayer life?

CHAPTER 3

SEPARATION ESCALATION

"When God created the heavens and the earth, it's likely that He never had separation in mind. After bringing forth the earth, the waters, and the skies, the Creator began to populate them...

"Then came man. Singular. In the midst of the many, there was one. God knew immediately that His work was not done. One final great act of creation was necessary for this work to be declared good. 'And the Lord God said, "It is not good that man should be alone; I will make him a helper comparable to him"' (Genesis 2:18). God put Adam to sleep, reached in, and pulled out a rib. Then, with a word, He transformed Adam's spare rib into a prime rib. *Togetherness* given as a gift to humanity.

"Not only was there togetherness within humanity, but there was also a together-relationship between God and this pinnacle of His creation. God dwelled among men. There was perfect harmony and peace. This was what God intended; this is what God declared to be good."

The Day Approaching, pages 41-42

ADAM AND EVE
SEPARATE FROM GOD

According to Genesis 3:23-24, what happened to this togetherness when Adam and Eve fell into sin?

What are the primary effects of sin?

Isaiah 59:2—

Romans 3:10-11—

Romans 6:23—

1 Corinthians 6:9-10—

Is there anything we can do in our own power to escape the effects of sin? What do the following passages say?

Romans 3:19-26—

Ephesians 2:8-9—

Titus 3:4-5—

CAIN SEPARATES FROM HIS FAMILY

"When Cain killed his brother, Satan gained two victories. The first was destroying a life, and the second was destroying a family."

The Day Approaching, page 44

Consider the sins listed below. In what ways can these sins destroy a family?

Sexual immorality—

Substance abuse—

Physical or verbal abuse—

Lying—

Jealousy—

Contention or strife—

Selfish ambition—

NOAH SEPARATES FROM WICKEDNESS

What were people like in Noah's day (see Genesis 6:5)?

What was God's response (verse 6)?

Whom did God choose to spare from the flood (verses 18-20)?

What prompted God to choose Noah (verse 8)?

What prompted God to make salvation available to us (Titus 2:11)?

"The picture of the righteous being separated from the unrighteous world and lifted up to safety is something that we will see take place again when the Lord lifts us up to meet Him in the sky."

The Day Approaching, page 45

ABRAHAM SEPARATES FROM
ALL HE KNOWS

Read Genesis 12:1-3. What command did God give to Abraham?

What promises did God include in the command?

God told Abraham to leave his family and everything he knew, and to head for a distant land he had never seen—Abraham had no idea what to expect. Imagine yourself in Abraham's shoes. In what ways would that kind of move be difficult for you?

In terms of separating from sin—what kinds of sacrifices are necessary on our part to make that happen?

Following Jesus comes with a cost and can require painful decisions. What are some of the things that can hinder us from serving Him?

Why is it worthwhile for us to make that kind of sacrifice?

> "Our love for Jesus must be so great that our love for anyone
> else pales in comparison."
>
> *The Day Approaching*, page 46

MOSES SEPARATES FROM EGYPT

In the story about Moses, we see at least three separations take place—(1) Moses' departure from Egypt after he killed an Egyptian who was abusing a slave, (2) the Jewish people's release from a nation of idol-worshippers so that they might follow the one true God, and (3) the tribe of Levi's separation from the rest of Israel when they purged the camp of those who had been the worst offenders in the golden calf incident.

In all three cases, the separation God called for required total allegiance to him. It all comes down to whether you are on the Lord's side or not.

Read Joshua 24:15. What bold proclamation did Joshua give at the end of this verse?

What do you think a house that serves the Lord would look like?

Read Hebrews 11:24-26. What choice did Moses make? What did Moses consider to be "greater…than the treasures in Egypt"?

Read both Romans 8:18 and 1 Peter 1:3-4. How do Paul and Peter describe the glory and inheritance that await us in heaven?

On page 47 of *The Day Approaching* we read, "Sometimes God must separate us from the norm or the comfortable or the easy so He can prepare us to serve Him." Do you agree? Why?

THE CHURCH SEPARATES FROM THE LAW AND THE WORLD

One of the problems the early church faced was the fact that those from a Jewish background thought they still needed to observe certain Jewish traditions that no longer needed to be followed. And the Gentiles who came from thoroughly pagan cultures found it hard to leave behind their old lifestyles.

Both the Jews and Gentiles who received Christ as Savior and Lord found themselves facing tremendous pressure from their peers who had not yet become believers. For this reason, the cost of separation for Christ's sake was high.

Yet as Christians, we now have a "second family"—an international body of brothers and sisters in Christ!

Read Galatians 3:28, which talks about the inherent oneness we as believers have in Christ. With that in mind, what are some of the physical, cultural, and social traits that so easily divide people in today's culture?

What are some of the things that we as Christians share in common that help make us feel as though we truly are family?

THE CHURCH SEPARATES
FROM THE WORLD

The "Great Separation" refers to the setting apart of the church from the world—not in the sense of removing ourselves from the people around us, but living pure lives in the midst of a fallen culture.

Jesus calls us to live as "the salt of the earth" and "the light of the world" (Matthew 5:13-14). In what way does Jesus' admonishment help us to understand how we should—and shouldn't—relate to unbelievers?

What does Philippians 2:14-15 say about how we should live, and why?

ABIDING IN GOD'S WORD AS WE AWAIT CHRIST'S RETURN

See then that you walk circumspectly, not as fools but as wise, redeeming the time, because the days are evil. Therefore do not be unwise, but understand what the will of the Lord is (Ephesians 5:15-17).

"Are you separated to God, or are you separated to the world? Everyone is on one side or the other—there is no middle ground…By all appearances, the time is short. We must take seriously the role we've been given as ambassadors of Christ."

The Day Approaching, pages 49,54

What happens when we attempt to live in the "middle ground"?

An ambassador is a representative. In what ways can we excel as ambassadors for Christ?

Where do you see room for growth in the ways you represent Christ to a watching world?

CHAPTER 4

AN EXTENDED 70 WEEKS

"When we pray, God hears. When the Lord makes a promise, we can hold Him to it. When we pray a reminder to Him, as Daniel did, it is not because we think He may have forgotten. He's not looking at His calendar thinking, *I know I circled that date for a reason.* When we remind God of His promises, it is a statement of faith on our part. We are affirming that He is a God who always follows through with His commitments."

The Day Approaching, pages 60-61

DANIEL AND HIS BOOK

Read page 61 of *The Day Approaching*. How would you describe the first six chapters of Daniel?

The second six chapters?

ISRAEL IN TIME-OUT

Read Leviticus 25:1-4. What command did God give to the Israelites?

What was the purpose of this command?

According to Leviticus 26:32-35, what punishment did God say would occur if the people disobeyed? More specifically, what did God say He would do to the people?

And what would happen to the land?

> "The land would have its Sabbaths one way or another. If the Israelites refused to let the land rest, the Lord would refuse the Israelites the land until the Sabbaths were completed."
>
> *The Day Approaching,* page 59

In Daniel chapter 9, Daniel prayed to God, noting that according to the prophet Jeremiah, the 70-year exile that was designed to give the land its Sabbath rest was coming to an end. As Daniel prayed, the angel Gabriel came and confirmed that "seventy weeks [years] are determined for your people and for your holy city, to finish the transgression, to make an end of sins, to make reconciliation for iniquity, to bring in everlasting righteousness, to seal up vision and prophecy, and to anoint the Most Holy" (verse 24).

Through Gabriel's response, God was confirming that His prophecy about the 70 years of exile was being fulfilled—and that the prophesied time of punishment was indeed coming to an end.

> "God will fulfill His promises in His time and in His way, 100 percent of the time."
>
> *The Day Approaching,* page 61

THE APOCALYPSE OF DANIEL

Read Daniel 9:20-22. For what purpose had Gabriel come to Daniel, according to verse 22?

How quickly did God send Gabriel to respond to Daniel's prayer (verse 23)?

What promises do we find in the following passages about God's response when we pray to Him?

Philippians 4:6-7—

Hebrews 4:16—

James 1:5—

1 John 5:14—

"Our God, who knows the words we are going to say even before we say them, is less concerned about what comes out of our mouths than what is in our hearts."

The Day Approaching, page 63

DANIEL'S 70 WEEKS

"The weeks Gabriel talks about are not made up of seven days, but seven years. So the 70 weeks actually refers to a period of 490 years—70 x 7."

The Day Approaching, page 64

According to Daniel 9:25-26, how much time will pass from the command to restore Jerusalem to the time the Messiah comes and is cut off?

When was the command given for Jerusalem to be rebuilt (Nehemiah 2:1-6)?

Doing the math, the "seven weeks and sixty-two weeks" mentioned in Daniel 9:25 add up to 476 solar years. When we start from the month of Nisan in 445 BC and add 476 solar years, we arrive at Palm Sunday in AD 31.

What does this mathematical precision tell you about God Himself?

What does this precision tell you about Bible prophecy?

THE MISSING SEVENTIETH WEEK

Quickly review pages 68-71 in *The Day Approaching*, then answer the following questions:

What analogy did Bible teacher Clarence Larkin come up with to explain what happens between week 69 and week 70 in Daniel's 70-weeks prophecy?

What does the valley between Mount 69 and Mount 70 represent?

What will happen when we reach the base of the second mountain, or Mount 70?

According to Daniel 9:24, what are the six reasons for these prophesied 70 weeks?

Of those six, when did Jesus accomplish the first three?

When will Jesus accomplish the second three?

"The day of the seventieth week is approaching. God is going to deal once again with Israel. The valley between the peaks was a desert for the Jews. But then came 1948, and suddenly Israel was back home. God has brought Israel back—and now we are waiting for Him to pour out His Spirit upon the Jewish people. What a glorious day it will be when we see mass repentance and reconciliation between the Lord and His chosen nation! Lift up your eyes—the base of the mountain is almost at our feet, and the path of the church is nearing the end."

The Day Approaching, page 71

ABIDING IN GOD'S WORD
AS WE AWAIT CHRIST'S RETURN

> Thus says the Lord GOD: "I do not do this for your sake, O house of Israel, but for My holy name's sake, which you have profaned among the nations wherever you went. And I will sanctify My great name…and the nations shall know that I am the Lord," says the Lord GOD, "when I am hallowed in you before their eyes. For I will take you from among the nations, gather you out of all countries, and bring you into your own land" (Ezekiel 36:22-24).

For whose sake did God bring the people of Israel back to their own land?

What had the people of Israel done to God's name?

By keeping His promise to Israel, what did God say He would do to His name?

What would the nations know when they saw the people of Israel return to their land?

Every time God fulfills a prophecy, He sanctifies His name—He calls attention to the fact He alone is God and thus brings glory to Himself. In what ways does God's ability to prophesy the future—*and* fulfill those prophecies—affect your view of Him?

CHAPTER 5

THE LONG SHADOW
OF THE PASSOVER

"Through His prophets and writers, the Lord often used shadows to represent something of substance—sort of like ancient literary holograms that represent something or someone real. The writer of Hebrews tells us that many years ago there was an earthly sanctuary that was set up for sacrifices offered to the Lord...

"But as wonderful as this first temple and sacrificial system were, we are told that they were only 'symbolic for the present time' (Hebrews 9:9). They were only the shadow—an illustration of a greater reality. That greater reality is found in the heavenly temple and sacrifice of Jesus Christ."

The Day Approaching, page 74

This shadow/substance pairing is the essence of Bible prophecy. A shadow will point to a coming substance or fulfillment. Let's look at one example:

Read Isaiah 7:14. What is prophesied here?

Now read Matthew 1:21-25. What is the fulfillment?

Can you think of two or three other shadow/substance pairs that appear in the Bible? List the passages here.

THE SHADOW OF THE FEASTS

In recent decades, there has come a growing trend toward churches wanting to observe the feasts of the Old Testament. Are these churches focusing on the shadow or the substance?

Which do you think God wants us to focus on, and why?

"The feasts are a shadow; the substance is Christ. The feasts have done their job; let's now focus on the real thing."

The Day Approaching, page 76

While there is no need to celebrate the feasts, what advantage is there in studying about them?

What ultimate purpose did the feasts serve for the people of Israel?

THE BEGINNING OF THE PASSOVER

What instructions did God give in Exodus 12:3-7?

Why did God command that the lamb be kept with the family for four days? What point did He want to make to His people?

What did God say He would do on the night that the Israelites were to put the lamb's blood on their doorposts (verses 12-13)?

What specifically determined whether the Lord would kill—or not kill—the firstborn humans or creatures in any given home?

What does Hebrews 9:22 say is necessary for us to receive forgiveness for our sins?

SHADOW AND SUBSTANCE IN THE PASSOVER

What did John the Baptist say in John 1:29?

The sacrificial lamb in Egypt served as a shadow of what future greater reality, according to 1 Corinthians 5:7?

Read Hebrews 10:11-12. What was the main difference between the sacrifices made by the Old Testament priests, and the sacrifice offered up by Christ?

What does verse 14 go on to tell us?

What does this tell us about the security of the salvation that Christ made possible for us?

Quickly review pages 80-81 in *The Day Approaching*. What kind of bread were the Jewish people to make before their long journey—that is, what one ingredient were they to leave out?

To make sure future generations of Israelites remembered how quickly the people had to leave Egypt, what feast did God institute to accompany Passover?

What did the purging of leaven symbolize in the lives of the people?

Who is the ultimate example of the unleavened life?

ABIDING IN GOD'S WORD
AS WE AWAIT CHRIST'S RETURN

Having boldness to enter the Holiest by the blood
of Jesus, by a new and living way which He con-
secrated for us, through the veil, that is, His flesh,
and having a High Priest over the house of God,
let us draw near with a true heart in full assurance
of faith, having our hearts sprinkled from an evil
conscience and our bodies washed with pure water.
Let us hold fast the confession of our hope without
wavering, for He who promised is faithful. And
let us consider one another in order to stir up love
and good works, not forsaking the assembling of
ourselves together, as is the manner of some, but
exhorting one another, and so much the more as
you see the Day approaching (Hebrews 10:19-25).

Hebrews chapter 10 closes with a reminder of how we ought
to respond to Christ's incredible sacrifice on our behalf. Three
times we are told "let us." What three things are we called to do?

1. Let us…

2. Let us…

3. Let us…

Which of these exhortations is particularly meaningful to you, and why?

CHAPTER 6

THE LONG SHADOW OF THE OTHER FEASTS

"The Passover was the first feast instituted, and it made a huge impact. It reminded the Hebrews of God's power and faithfulness, united them together as one people, and provided an opportunity for national worship. Although Passover was the first of the feasts, it was certainly not the last. Six more feasts were to follow—each one with its own rituals and its own purpose. And, like Passover, each of the other feasts had both a shadow component and the ultimate substance."

The Day Approaching, page 83

THE FEAST OF FIRSTFRUITS

How was the Feast of Firstfruits celebrated?

The feast itself was a shadow—what greater reality did the feast point to?

Jesus is called the firstfruits in 1 Corinthians 15:20. What does the use of the word *first* tell us?

What does 2 Corinthians 4:14 say? How much confidence can we have in that promise, and why?

THE FEAST OF WEEKS (PENTECOST)

How many days after the Feast of Firstfruits did the Jewish nation observe the Feast of Weeks (Pentecost)?

What happened on the Day of Pentecost as described in Acts 2:1-4?

What reality or substance did God bring about on that day, which the people had never experienced before?

What two things does the sealing of the Holy Spirit do?

Read John 10:28 and Romans 8:35-39. What assurance are we given in these verses?

THE FEAST OF TRUMPETS

Briefly describe the trumpets used to observe the Feast of Trumpets.

What was the purpose of the trumpets?

What did Jesus want us to learn from the fig tree (Matthew 24:32-33)?

What miraculous event occurred to Israel that indicates the fig tree has budded?

What two witnesses is God using to warn people that something is about to happen?

THE DAY OF ATONEMENT

What did God mean when He used the term "afflict your souls" in Leviticus 23:27?

What did God want His people to recognize on the Day of Atonement?

What does Zechariah 12:10 say will happen in the future?

And what will be the result, according to Romans 11:26?

THE FEAST OF TABERNACLES

During this week-long celebration, the people of Israel would come to Jerusalem to set up temporary shelters, or tabernacles. What was the reason for setting up these booths?

What is the substance or reality seen in this feast (Zechariah 14:16)?

ARE THE FESTIVALS FULFILLED?

Which of the feasts have been fulfilled, which is being carried out now, and which are yet to come?

ABIDING IN GOD'S WORD AS WE AWAIT CHRIST'S RETURN

If the trumpet makes an uncertain sound, who will prepare for battle? (1 Corinthians 14:8).

Trumpets are used as warnings and signals that someone is coming and something is about to happen. With that in mind, ask yourself: What kind of trumpet am I?

1. In what ways can you serve as a trumpet?

2. Write a short list of four or five names of those who immediately come to mind as individuals who need Jesus Christ—coworkers, friends, family members. What specific prayers can you lift up for these people, and what one or two steps can you take to serve more as a trumpet in their lives?

CHAPTER 7

THE VIEW FROM THE MIDDLE EAST

"Is the Middle East really out of control? Could it be that instead of wild mayhem, what we are witnessing is all part of a larger plan? Is it possible that even though we don't see an engineer in the driver's seat, there is still someone there steering this train?

"The answer is yes. Not only is it possible, but that is exactly what's happening. The runaway train of the Middle East has not run away at all. It is 100 percent on course, locked into a rail line that was laid out for it many centuries ago."

The Day Approaching, pages 100-101

EXPECT THE UNEXPECTED

As the world spins seemingly out of control, we may find ourselves tempted to think that maybe God isn't really sovereign after all. But what do the following verses tell us?

Deuteronomy 3:24—

1 Samuel 2:10—

Job 9:10—

Proverbs 21:1—

Isaiah 43:13—

Jeremiah 32:27—

"We may think the wicked are doing great while the righteous suffer, but that is only because we can't see the world through God's eyes. He has the eternal view."

The Day Approaching, page 102

Can you give a specific example of a time when you struggled because the wicked seemed to have everything going in their favor?

What helped you to have a right perspective about the temporary success of the wicked as compared to the eternal rewards of a righteous life?

What was God able to teach you through the experience?

In what ways do the following verses encourage you?

Romans 8:18—

2 Corinthians 4:17-18—

THE JEWS? REALLY?

What do the following verses affirm about God?

Deuteronomy 10:14—

1 Chronicles 29:11—

Psalm 89:11—

In light of what those verses say, do we have any reason to be anxious about what is happening in the world around us? Why or why not?

It was God who chose to work through Abraham, as well as through the nation of Israel. He also chose to work through the disciples, whose weaknesses are made evident to us in the New Testament. Similarly, God has chosen to work through you even with your imperfections. What can we learn from God's willingness to work through flawed vessels?

How does God's willingness to work through weak instruments affect your perspective of Him?

THE LAND OF ISRAEL? REALLY?

God also chose to do His work in a specific region of the world—the Middle East. Why was this such a strategic place for God to announce His existence to the world?

Read what Joseph said in Genesis 50:19-20. Share an example from your own life of a time when evil done against you was used by God to bring about a positive result.

MUSLIM VS. MUSLIM

What is the key reason for the conflict that occurs between the two main factions within Islam?

Israel is enjoying unprecedented prosperity and security in the midst of all the turmoil in the Middle East. What does that tell you about God?

PSALM 83 TO EZEKIEL 38

What kind of threat is made against Israel in Psalm 83:2-4?

If Satan had been able to successfully use past world powers or the present Arab nations to wipe out Israel, what would that say about God?

What do the following passages promise about Israel?

Genesis 12:3—

Leviticus 26:44—

Isaiah 27:12-13—

ABIDING IN GOD'S WORD
AS WE AWAIT CHRIST'S RETURN

Can a woman forget her nursing child,
and not have compassion on the son of her womb?
Surely they may forget,
yet I will not forget you.
See, I have inscribed you on the palms of My hands;
your walls are continually before Me
(Isaiah 49:15-16).

"God is in absolute control in the Middle East, carrying out His plans and fulfilling His promises. He has brought the Jews out of the period of Psalm 83. The day of Ezekiel 38 is fast approaching. This is even more evident as we go from the Middle East as a whole and zoom in on Israel in particular."

The Day Approaching, page 113

In what ways do you perceive the world around us is out of control? Come up with two or three specific examples.

How might God be working behind the scenes in those situations for His ultimate greater good?

CHAPTER 8

THE VIEW FROM ISRAEL

"Where is God in Israel? That's a question I often get asked, particularly by those who want to write off the modern nation as no different than any other country. It seems that these days, the only God that is evident as you wander around Jerusalem is the Old Testament Jehovah of Judaism, the angry Allah of Islam, or the old-school Adonai of Orthodoxy. Sure, if you look hard enough, you'll find evangelical Christian churches scattered here and there. But they are few and far between.

"Of greater concern, however, is the general lack of attention to God on the national scene. In many ways, Israel appears to be a secular state with a thin coat of religiosity—an atheist in rabbi's clothing."

The Day Approaching, page 115

Israel's spiritual state shouldn't surprise us. What do the following passages say is true of all people, no matter what their background?

Psalm 53:2-3—

Romans 3:10-11—

When it came to God's chosen people, what was the apostle Paul's deep longing, according to Romans 9:1-3 and 10:1?

What does Romans 11:25 say has happened to Israel, and what promise does God give for Israel's future in verse 26?

Read Zechariah 12:10 and Isaiah 46:13. What additional insights do these verses give about God's future work in the hearts of the Jewish people?

A LOOK AT ISRAEL TODAY

Based on what you read on pages 116-118 of *The Day Approaching*, what are a couple of examples that show the incredible transformation that has taken place in Israel?

What was the land like at the turn of the nineteenth century, and what do people see today?

What did God say would happen to Israel, according to Ezekiel 36:8-9?

When you do an online search of "Silicon Wadi" and do a quick skim of the articles that appear, what is your overall impression of where Israel stands today in terms of modern technology?

THE MUSLIM INVASION

Where are many Muslims fleeing to, and why?

What has been the result of the open-border policies in Western Europe?

Why does it make sense for Israel to exercise great caution and protect its status as the only truly democratic and non-Muslim entity in the entire Middle East?

THE TRIALS OF THE ARAB WORLD

What was the general result of the Arab Spring?

What Arab nations have begun to develop more favorable relations with Israel?

ISRAEL'S EXPANDING RELATIONSHIPS

Review pages 122-124 and cite a couple examples of ways that Israel's influence continues to grow.

Who gets the credit for Israel's incredible restoration and achievements, according to Ezekiel 37:13-14?

GOD IS IN CONTROL

Read Psalm 2:2-3. What insights does this passage give about the way world rulers perceive their power?

How does God respond to their perception, according to verse 4?

What does Proverbs 21:1 tell us about God and world leaders?

"God is in control of the Middle East, and He is in control of Israel. That alone should be enough to bring peace to our hearts, no matter how bad the craziness we see on our television screens at night.

"Not only should we not be afraid, we should be encouraged. Everything is playing out exactly as God said it would."

The Day Approaching, page 126

When it appears as if the world is falling apart and God is nowhere to be found, how do you remind yourself that everything is indeed going according to God's plan?

ABIDING IN GOD'S WORD
AS WE AWAIT CHRIST'S RETURN

> I am God, and there is no other;
> I am God, and there is no one like Me,
> declaring the end from the beginning,
> and from ancient times things which have not
>   been done,
> saying, "My purpose will be established,
> and I will accomplish all My good pleasure"…
> Truly I have spoken; truly I will bring it to pass.
> I have planned it, surely I will do it
>   (Isaiah 46:9-11).

In what ways are you encouraged as you read the words of Isaiah 46:9-11?

Take some time now to pray to the Lord and express your gratitude and trust in His plans not only for the whole world, but for your own life.

CHAPTER 9

WHEN THE RESTRAINER STOPS RESTRAINING

"There is a restrainer in place right now, held secure by the Lord. But it will not remain there forever. A time is coming when the restrainer will be removed. On that day, people had better run for high ground, because devastation will pour down on them quickly."

The Day Approaching, page 128

THE COMING APOSTASY

Read 2 Thessalonians 2:1-3. In verses 1-2, what assurance did Paul give to the believers at Thessalonica?

According to verse 3, what must happen first before Jesus returns?

What does *apostasy* refer to?

Why does it make sense that false teachings that originate *within* the church can be more dangerous than false teachings from outside?

Second Thessalonians 2:6-8 says, "Now you know what is restraining, that he may be revealed in his own time. For the mystery of lawlessness is already at work; only He who now restrains will do so until He is taken out of the way. And then the lawless one will be revealed."

What does this passage say about "the mystery of lawlessness"?

What must be taken out of the way before the "lawless one"—the Antichrist—is revealed?

THE RESTRAINER REVEALED

In Genesis 6:7-8 we read, "The LORD said, 'I will destroy man...But Noah found grace in the eyes of the LORD.'" And in Romans 6:23, we are told, "The wages of sin is death, but the gift of God is eternal life in Christ Jesus our Lord."

In both verses, circle the word "but." What key shift occurs as we go from the first half of each verse to the second half?

> "God is not looking for an excuse to destroy; He is looking for an excuse to preserve and to bless."
>
> *The Day Approaching,* page 132

In what ways have you found the above-stated principle to be true in your own life?

Read 2 Thessalonians 2:9-12. How extensive will the Antichrist's deception be?

When Abraham negotiated with God about sparing Sodom and Gomorrah, we see God's willingness to hold back judgment for the sake of even ten righteous people. According to 2 Peter 3:9, why is God "longsuffering toward us"?

"God's judgment is ready for this world. However, He is holding it back until the time is right and He removes His church. Thus, the restrainer is God's presence in His people who are in this world. We are His ambassadors. We are His watchmen. When people see us, they see Christ. And when they see Christ, they see the Father."

The Day Approaching, pages 137-138

THE CHURCH'S ROLE IN RESTRAINING

In Matthew 5:13-14, Jesus said that we as believers are "the salt of the earth…the light of the world."

Describe two or three ways in which we can intentionally and proactively be salt and light to those around us.

When people see you, how well do you think they can see Jesus?

Can you think of one or two areas in your life where you could improve on letting Christ shine through you?

What kind of life are we called to live, according to 1 Timothy 2:1-2?

Why would doing this have such a great impact on others?

THE REMOVAL OF THE RESTRAINER

First Thessalonians 4:16-18 describes the rapture. When Christians have been removed from earth, the restrainer will be gone. What do you think will be among the more noticeable changes in the absence of any Christian influence whatsoever?

According to Hosea 5:15, what will affliction drive the people of Israel to do?

Judgment will come after the restrainer is removed. In what two ways will people respond to God's wrath?

ABIDING IN GOD'S WORD
AS WE AWAIT CHRIST'S RETURN

> The Lord is not slack concerning His promise, as
> some count slackness, but is longsuffering toward
> us, not willing that any should perish but that all
> should come to repentance (2 Peter 3:9).

God is longsuffering—He's patient. As we consider just how
evil a world we live in, it's amazing that God has been willing to hold back His judgment for so long. Do you exhibit
that same kind of patience to unbelievers around you? Why
is that so important?

> I exhort...that supplications, prayers, intercessions,
> and giving of thanks be made for all men, for kings
> and all who are in authority (1 Timothy 2:1-2).

How are you doing at praying for the people around you,
including those in positions of authority? What are some of
the benefits you think we could experience by making a habit
of praying for others, including our government leaders?

Take some time now to lift up such a prayer.

CHAPTER 10

MEANWHILE, UP IN HEAVEN...

"When the plane is cruising through the thick masses of water droplets and moisture beads make their way across the window panes, I'm smiling. I'm thinking of the future. I dream of the day when I will be inside the clouds yet outside of the plane. That is where I will meet my Lord face to face for the first time. Then, after I am gathered with the rest of the church on that blessed day and we are received by the Savior, we will go up with Him, and not come back down. Seven years will go by before we'll see the surface of the earth again. During that time, there is a lot that will be taking place below the clouds, as well as above."

The Day Approaching, page 144

SET YOUR MIND ON THINGS ABOVE

Colossians 3:1-2 says, "Seek those things which are above, where Christ is, sitting at the right hand of God. Set your mind on things above, not on things on the earth." The phrase "set your mind" speaks of deliberately and intentionally focusing your mind on the things of God. For us to have heavenly thoughts requires that we fill our minds with Scripture. Read the following passages, and write, in your own words, what it means to "set your mind on things above":

Romans 8:5-6—

Romans 12:2—

Philippians 4:8—

What do you envision would be the positive side effects of making it a habit to "set your mind on things above"?

As a Christian, you have a new identity in Christ—you are a new person. What do the following verses tell us about who we are as believers?

2 Corinthians 5:17—

Philippians 3:20—

Colossians 3:3—

Based on the above Scripture verses, if we are in Christ and we are new creations, how should that affect…

our thoughts?

our emotions and attitudes?

our behavior?

FROM CORRUPTIBLE TO INCORRUPTIBLE

One of the best ways to focus on things above is to focus on Christ Himself. He is the supreme example of one who had His mind set on heavenly things. In Romans 8:29, we read that God is working in us to conform us "to the image of His Son." In a practical sense, what does it mean to follow Christ's example?

As 1 Corinthians 15:51-53 says, we live in corruptible bodies afflicted by sin and the aging process. What are some of the negative effects we experience as a result of living in fallen and corruptible bodies?

What are some of the positives we can look forward to when we receive our future incorruptible bodies?

WHAT WE WILL DO IN HEAVEN

After we are raptured to heaven, seven years will go by before Christ returns to earth in full glory to set up His millennial kingdom. In John 14:2-3, Jesus gives us a clue about our future dwelling place during those seven years: "In My Father's house are many mansions; if it were not so, I would have told you. I go to prepare a place for you. And if I go and prepare a place for you, I will come again and receive you to Myself; that where I am, there you may be also."

What did Jesus say in John 14:2-3 that reveals just how much He loves you?

In what ways can you imagine your heavenly home being more fulfilling and satisfying than your earthly home?

Upon arriving in heaven, "we must appear before the judgment seat of Christ, that each one may receive the things done in the body, according to what he has done, whether good or bad" (2 Corinthians 5:8-10). The believer's judgment is not about salvation—once we are saved, we are always saved. Rather, God will examine our intentions and our works—the manner in which we served Him while on earth. What assurances do the following passages give about the permanence of our salvation?

Romans 8:1—

Romans 8:35-39—

Ephesians 1:13-14—

In 1 Corinthians 3:12, our works are described as either "gold, silver, precious stones," or "wood, hay, straw." Which works will survive the fire that test each person's works?

What kinds of works do you think gold, silver, and precious stones represent?

What kinds of works do you think wood, hay, and straw represent?

We may find ourselves feeling nervous or afraid about this coming judgment for all believers, but really, we should look forward to it with joy. Why do you think that is?

What can we do to ensure we look forward to this event with joy? As you answer, consider what Paul wrote in Acts 24:16: "I myself always strive to have a conscience without offense toward God and men."

In what ways can you show Christ—Your Savior—that you are living in anticipation of His return?

ABIDING IN GOD'S WORD AS WE AWAIT CHRIST'S RETURN

> Do you not know that those who run in a race all run, but one receives the prize? Run in such a way that you may obtain it. And everyone who competes for the prize is temperate in all things. Now they do it to obtain a perishable crown, but we for an imperishable crown. Therefore I run thus: not with uncertainty. Thus I fight: not as one who beats the air. But I discipline my body and bring it into subjection (1 Corinthians 9:24-27).

In what manner are we called to run the Christian race?

What kind of prize are we pursuing?

How can we know, from the words above, that this will not be an easy race?

What parallels do you see between the kind of discipline the world's best athletes need so they can stay competitive, and the kind of discipline we need as believers?

CHAPTER 11

THE MILLENNIUM—
THE THOUSAND YEARS BEGIN

"There is good news and bad news when it comes to the millennium. The good news is that it is wonderful beyond our imagination. Peace and tranquility will be the new world order as Christ reigns from Jerusalem. The bad news is that we aren't in the millennium yet."

The Day Approaching, page 158

CHARACTERISTICS OF
THE MILLENNIAL KINGDOM

What will life be like in the millennial kingdom, according to Isaiah 65:18-23?

What specific traits will characterize this kingdom?

Isaiah 2:4—

Isaiah 9:7—

Isaiah 61:11—

What are some of the physical blessings we will enjoy in the millennial kingdom?

Isaiah 11:6-7—

Isaiah 30:23-24—

Isaiah 65:20—

What are some of the spiritual blessings we'll experience?

Psalm 22:27—

Psalm 85:10-11—

Zechariah 2:10-11—

Based on what you've learned about the characteristics of the millennial kingdom, why can we be certain that we are *not* currently living in this kingdom, as some people claim?

THE PROBLEMS WITH AMILLENNIALISM

Amillennialists believe that Jesus is currently reigning over the world from heaven through the church. From their perspective, because Jesus is on His heavenly throne, that means that His kingdom has come.

Yet even a casual glance at the world around us reveals that the amillennial perspective simply doesn't make sense. In addition to the scriptural evidence we looked at a moment ago, what commonsense evidence around us refutes the idea that Christ is actually ruling over the entire globe?

Amillennialists say the millennial kingdom began at the cross, and it will continue until the second coming of Christ. However, Christ's first coming took place 2,000 years ago, and the Latin word for thousand is *mille*, which refers to only 1,000. What does Revelation 20:1-7 say about the length of the millennial kingdom, and how many times is this number stated?

Amillennialists say the number 1,000 in Revelation 20 shouldn't be taken literally, but rather, that it is simply figurative speech that means "a long time." But what is the problem with their argument that Revelation 20 is to be interpreted figuratively when the passage doesn't give any indication it should be taken figuratively? What would be the danger of arbitrarily interpreting other passages of Scripture in symbolic or figurative ways when there's no clear reason to do so?

A LITERAL KINGDOM

"The millennium will be a literal kingdom in which Christ reigns for 1,000 years from a physical throne in Jerusalem. There will literally be actual changes in the physical realm, the spiritual realm, and the natural realm. I use the word literally on purpose because the changes are spelled out to us in the Word of God—spoken by the prophets and witnessed by the apostle John...

"When those 1,000 years begin, you and I won't be disembodied spirits hovering in an ethereal world. We will get to experience every sight, sound, taste, and smell as we physically experience Jesus Christ's reign on this earth."

The Day Approaching, page 169

Read Isaiah 9:7. What stands out the most to you in this verse, and why?

ABIDING IN GOD'S WORD AS WE AWAIT CHRIST'S RETURN

The mountain of the LORD's house shall be established on top of the mountains, and shall be exalted above the hills; and all the nations shall flow to it. Many people shall come and say, "Come, let us go up to the mountain of the LORD, to the house of the God of Jacob; He will teach us His ways, and we shall walk in His paths" (Isaiah 2:2-3).

It shall come to pass that everyone who is left of all the nations which came against Jerusalem shall go up from year to year to worship the King, the LORD of hosts and to keep the Feast of Tabernacles (Zechariah 14:16).

During the millennium, all the nations of the earth will truly live in subjection to Christ's rule, and the peoples will come to Jerusalem regularly to worship Him. In contrast to earthly kings and government officials, Christ will reign with perfect wisdom, love, justice, and righteousness. What are some of the reasons you're looking forward to living in Christ's 1,000-year kingdom?

CHAPTER 12

THE MILLENNIUM—WHO'S LEFT IN THE NEIGHBORHOOD?

"With the arrival of the millennium will come great changes... There will be peace on earth. All God's creatures will dwell together in harmony. The Lord Himself will be among His people, and they will worship Him in person. The world will have a nostalgic quality to it, similar to what was once enjoyed in the Garden of Eden."

The Day Approaching, page 171

THE CONFUSION ABOUT THE MILLENNIUM

Based on Ezekiel 34:23-24 and Jeremiah 30:9, the Jewish people are expecting a new King David—a human Messiah—to reign over them in the future. They completely miss the fact that Jesus, who came 2,000 years ago, is the Messiah they've been waiting for. Because Jesus didn't fit their expectations of what the Messiah would do, they didn't recognize Him at His first coming.

Understanding the Two Resurrections

Jesus is "the firstfruits of those who have fallen asleep" (1 Corinthians 15:20). What does the fact Jesus is called "the firstfruits" reveal to us?

Read 1 Thessalonians 4:15-17. What two groups of people will be taken up in the rapture portion of the first resurrection?

Which group will be taken up first, and which will be taken up second?

Who else will be taken up in the first resurrection, according to the following passages?

Revelation 11:11-12 (the midpoint of the tribulation)—

Daniel 12:1-2 (the end of the tribulation)—

Revelation 20:4-6 (the end of the tribulation)—

Up till now, we've seen that all *believers* will have part in the first resurrection, though in varying stages. When will the "rest of the dead"—or *unbelievers*—be raised, according to Revelation 20:5?

Let's read Revelation 20:11-15 carefully:

> I saw a great white throne and Him who sat on it, from whose face the earth and the heaven fled away. And there was found no place for them. And I saw the dead, small and great, standing before God, and books were opened. And another book was opened, which is the Book of Life. And the dead were judged according to their works, by the things which were written in the books. The sea gave up the dead who were in it, and Death and Hades delivered up the dead who were in them. And they were judged, each one according to his works. Then Death and Hades were cast into the lake of fire. This is the second death. And anyone not found written in the Book of Life was cast into the lake of fire.

This event is commonly known as the Great White Throne Judgment. Do you get the sense that anyone can escape this judgment? Why?

What are these unbelievers judged "according to"?

What will happen to anyone "not found written in the Book of Life"?

Between the first and second resurrections, every single person who has ever lived will be raised up. Those taken up in the first resurrection will experience eternity with Christ, and those of the second resurrection will be forever separated from Him.

Understanding How the Bible Uses Typology

In simple terms, a type is a foreshadow of something greater to come.

What were the Passover lambs sacrificed in Egypt (in Exodus 12) a type of (see John 1:29)?

What are some of the ways King David was a type of Christ (what similarities do they share)?

2 Samuel 7:8-9 and Philippians 2:5-10—

2 Samuel 8:15 and Isaiah 9:7—

1 Chronicles 22:10 and Luke 1:32-33—

A JERUSALEM LANDING

Read Zechariah 14:3-4. At what geographical location will Jesus return to earth to set up His throne in the millennial kingdom?

According to Zechariah 12:10 and Hosea 5:15, how will the Jewish people of that future day react when they see Jesus?

What result did the apostle Paul promise in Romans 11:26-27?

What does Jeremiah 30:9 say the Jewish inhabitants of the millennial kingdom will do?

What kind of relationship will exist between God and His chosen people (Jeremiah 31:33-34)?

"What a day it will be when those divine feet touch Earth once again. The resurrected church will return with her husband, and the Jewish people will recognize their Messiah."

The Day Approaching, page 183

ABIDING IN GOD'S WORD
AS WE AWAIT CHRIST'S RETURN

> For unto us a Child is born,
> unto us a Son is given;
> and the government will be upon His shoulder.
> And His name will be called
> Wonderful, Counselor, Mighty God,
> Everlasting Father, Prince of Peace.
> Of the increase of His government and peace
> there will be no end (Isaiah 9:6-7).

Based on the words of Isaiah 9:6, what kind of king will Jesus be?

What will be true about His government, according to verse 7?

Sometimes we find it difficult to subject to secular governing authorities, as commanded in Romans 13:1-2. Because these authorities are fallen and sinful humans, they make imperfect leaders. How easy or difficult do you think it will be for us to subject ourselves to Christ's rule, and why?

CHAPTER 13

THE MILLENNIUM—MORE THAN A LONG TIME-OUT

"What will Jerusalem look like during those 1,000 years? Who will be in the millennial kingdom, and how might they interact with one another? What is the purpose of the millennium? And why is it so vitally important that we study all this today?"

The Day Approaching, page 186

JERUSALEM IN THE MILLENNIUM

The Jerusalem we know today is the same Jerusalem that will exist in Israel during the millennial kingdom—the New Jerusalem won't descend from heaven until God has created the new heaven and new earth. However, there will be a new building that doesn't exist today—what building is that (Ezekiel 47:1)?

What will flow from the threshold of that building (verse 1)?

What effect will this water have, according to verses 8-9?

Read verse 12. What are some of the special characteristics of the trees that line the banks of the river?

List here the four temples mentioned on pages 188-189 of *The Day Approaching*. Why will there be no need for a temple when the new heavens and new earth arrive (Revelation 21:22)?

WHAT WILL WE DO DURING THE MILLENNIUM?

What does Revelation 20:6 say our primary role will be during the millennium?

What two groups of people who survive the tribulation will be admitted into the millennial kingdom (see page 189 of *The Day Approaching*)?

When Jesus returns at His second coming, what will He first do before setting up His kingdom (see Matthew 25:31-33)?

Those who survive the tribulation will enter the millennium in their earthly bodies, meaning sin will still exist and though people will live longer, they will still die. Those of us who have our glorified bodies, however, will not. This means the millennium will be a time of immortals interacting with mortals.

From a global standpoint, the millennium will be a time when national Israel will know the fullness of all God's promises to her, and the Gentile nations will enjoy the overflow of blessings that emanate from Christ's reign. All the peoples of the earth will travel to Jerusalem to worship the Lord, whose kingdom will be characterized by righteousness, holiness, obedience, justice, and love.

One major difference we'll experience is that the Lord Himself will be in our midst—which will have an incredible impact on our spiritual lives. We will live daily in the presence of Christ, and "the earth shall be full of the knowledge of the LORD as the waters cover the sea" (Isaiah 11:9).

Today, as Christians and within the church, we worship Jesus though we cannot see Him. In what ways do you think our worship might change when, during the millennial kingdom, we will live in Christ's visible presence?

WHY DO WE EVEN NEED A MILLENNIUM?

According to John 3:17, what was the reason for Jesus' first coming?

In Acts 17:30-31, what does Paul say will be the purpose of Jesus' return?

"Notice the qualifier that describes the kind of judgment Christ will bring. When He judges, it will be 'in righteousness.' If God is going to judge the world on this basis, He will want to make sure that His righteousness has been clearly on display (Isaiah 11; 61). The truth was preached at His first coming, and will be displayed at His second coming. In the peace and beauty of the millennium, no one will be able to miss the evidences of God's character. It will be on exhibit in nature and amongst the nations."

The Day Approaching, page 193

Even when God's full righteousness is on display, people will still rebel against Him. How do we see this rejection manifest in...

Zechariah 14:16-19?

Revelation 20:7-10?

Ultimately, the millennium will reveal that even under God's perfect and righteous reign, the hearts of mortal, fallen people are still bent toward sin and rebellion. The millennium will serve as final proof that God's saving grace is the one and only answer for sin. Merely living in a perfect environment isn't enough; only a total transformation of the inner person by God Himself can bring true change.

Read Revelation 20:7-10. What will Satan do at the end of Christ's 1,000-year kingdom?

How will God respond?

Now read Revelation 20:11-15, which describes the last event that will take place before eternity begins. Who will be present at this judgment?

What will be the verdict for every person at this judgment, and why?

As you consider this final judgment scene, what are your thoughts in response to the following passages?

Luke 19:13—

Ephesians 5:15-16—

1 Thessalonians 5:2—

2 Timothy 4:1-2—

> "The time is short. We must be about our Father's business."
>
> *The Day Approaching,* page 196

WHY DO WE NEED TO STUDY THE MILLENNIUM?

What two reasons are given for the importance of studying about the millennium (see pages 196-197 of *The Day Approaching*)?

—

—

Are you a believer? If not, do you recognize that procrastinating the decision to receive Christ as your Savior makes you vulnerable to eternal separation from God? As 2 Corinthians 6:2 says, "Behold, now is the accepted time; behold, now is the day of salvation." Give your heart to Christ and invite Him into your life as Savior and Lord so that you can be assured of a place in His millennial kingdom.

ABIDING IN GOD'S WORD
AS WE AWAIT CHRIST'S RETURN

> They lived and reigned with Christ for a thousand years (Revelation 20:4).

In what manner do the following passages say we are to carry out our service to the Lord?

Colossians 3:23-24—

1 Corinthians 15:58—

Our service here on earth is getting us ready for the responsibilities we will receive in heaven. In light of the passages mentioned above, in what ways can you grow in your service to God today?

What appeals to you most about the fact you'll serve and reign alongside Christ in His millennial kingdom?

CHAPTER 14

A LOOK AT THE BOOKS

"We are finally at the end of time. It's been a long journey that we've taken—starting way back in Genesis and arriving now at the grand finale of God's magnificent symphony of history. The old is about to give way to the new; the corrupt original is ready to be set aside so that the upgraded model can take its place. Heaven and Earth 2.0 are about to be revealed. But before we can take our final steps into eternity, there is some unfinished business. There are a few events that must take place, and sin must finally be dealt with once and for all."

The Day Approaching, page 199

THE GREAT DATA COLLECTOR

Skim pages 201-204, and list on the next page some of the information that our all-knowing God holds in His infinite mind:

—

—

—

—

—

—

—

—

—

—

Let's go back and take a closer look at three of the items on that list.

The Works of All People

It's common to hear unbelievers accuse God of being unfair. And there are even times when we who are Christians question God's fairness because things don't go the way we think they should. Like the psalmist, we may feel like crying out, "Will the Lord cast off forever? And will He be favorable no more? Has His mercy ceased forever? Has His promise failed forevermore?" (Psalm 77:7-8).

Read the following verses, and write what they tell you about God's knowledge, wisdom, and justice:

Deuteronomy 32:4—

Psalm 89:14—

Romans 11:33-36—

Hebrews 4:13—

In light of those passages, what can we know with certainty about the manner in which God will judge both believers and unbelievers?

How does the knowledge that God's judgment is absolutely fair help you with any anxiety you may have about facing God at the believers' judgment?

All Our Tears

Frequently when life becomes difficult, we feel as though we are far from God, or that He has forgotten us. Yet He is always with us, and He is very much aware of what we are going through. For example, Psalm 56:8 says, "You number my wanderings; put my tears into Your bottle; are they not in Your book?"

What additional assurances are we given in the following passages about God's presence in our lives when things go wrong?

2 Chronicles 16:9—

Psalm 46:1—

Isaiah 41:10—

Hebrews 13:5-6—

Every Godly Work

Scripture tells us not to give, pray, fast, or do any other work of righteousness for the purpose of being seen and noticed by others (Matthew 6:1-18). Our sole motivation should be to please God. Yet sometimes we may wonder if God is really paying attention to all that we do in service to Him and others. Perhaps we've been faithful, but from our earthly perspective, we feel as though we've received little or no reward for our labors. But God *does* notice.

Read Matthew 10:40-42. As Jesus recites different ways people served Him, what examples does He give?

What does this tell us about even the littlest things we do for Him?

What assurance are we given in Hebrews 6:10?

On this side of heaven, from our limited human perspective, we may feel there is little to no reward for our ministry labors. But what do we need to keep in mind, according to Matthew 16:27 and Revelation 22:12?

THE DUALITY OF THE BOOKS

What two births are spoken of in Scripture?

What two lives?

What two deaths?

What two resurrections?

And finally, what two books?

THE OPENING OF THE BOOKS

How does John the Revelator describe the scene at the Great White Throne Judgment in Revelation 20:12?

Will Christians be defendants or observers at this judgment? Explain.

Who are some of the specific people your heart breaks for as you read about this judgment?

How does this affect your resolve for reaching out to unbelievers whom you care about—while there is still time?

THE LAMB'S BOOK OF LIFE

"In the first set of books, the names are written in ink. In the second and greater book, the names are written in blood. And that blood is not our own—it is the blood of the perfect Lamb of God, who shed His own blood for the remission of our sins. It is this blood that has redeemed us for eternal life. This blood is permanent, indestructible, unable to be erased."

The Day Approaching, page 211

As we learned earlier, once saved, always saved. Take some time now to write a brief prayer of heartfelt gratitude to God for the remarkable gift He has given you—the gift of eternal life.

ANY DAY NOW

Hebrews 10:23-25 says,

Let us hold fast the confession of our hope without wavering, for He who promised is faithful. And let us consider one another in order to stir up love and good works, not forsaking the assembling of ourselves together, as is the manner of some, but exhorting one another, and so much the more as you see the Day approaching.

What specific actions are we called to as we see the Day approaching?

Note that God gives these calls to action in the context of an "any day now" passage. What does that tell you about the level of importance He ascribes to these actions?

What does verse 23 say about the God who makes promises to us?

How can we demonstrate to God that we are living with a true "any day now" mentality?

ABIDING IN GOD'S WORD
AS WE AWAIT CHRIST'S RETURN

He who testifies to these things says, "Surely
I am coming quickly." Amen. Even so, come,
Lord Jesus! (Revelation 22:20).

Imagine watching the life of a Christian who *isn't* eagerly
anticipating the Lord's return, and comparing that to the
life of a believer who is. What kinds of differences would
you see in their lives?

List three or four of the most significant benefits you have
gained from reading *The Day Approaching*, and share why
they mean so much to you.

FINAL THOUGHTS

"The Day is approaching. This is the Day when Jesus will rapture His church from the earth to meet Him. This is the Day of the Lord's judgment on sinners and the discipline of His people, Israel. This is the Day when Jesus will set foot upon the Mount of Olives, coming a second time to dwell on earth with His creation. This is the Day of the rule of the King of kings from His throne in Jerusalem. This is the Day of Satan's confinement, and of his eventual release and mankind's final rebellion. This is the Day of the Great White Throne judgment, when the sheep and the goats will be separated. And it is the Day of the new heaven and new earth, where we will enjoy the presence of the Lord forever."

The Day Approaching, page 213

What new truths have you learned from *The Day Approaching* that you never knew before?

As you have read what Scripture says about the rapture, second coming, and millennial kingdom, what has inspired you the most?

What has challenged you the most?

What life lessons are you most excited about applying from your study of *The Day Approaching*, and why?

In what ways can you use the knowledge you've gained from *The Day Approaching* to benefit the unbelievers in your life?

The believers?

As you go through the everyday routines of life, it is all too easy to become absorbed with the present and to be forgetful about living in full anticipation of Christ's return. In what ways can you make a deliberate effort to live with a constant awareness of what is to come?

As you consider the incredible future God has planned for you, what are you most thankful for?

In closing, take some time now to pray to God and express your gratitude to Him for His abounding goodness and grace.